The Chance to Dance

Written by Sandy Roydhouse
Illustrated by Xiangyi Mo and Jingwen Wang

China

Contents

Who Is Li Cunxin?

Li Cunxin is a world-famous ballet dancer. He was born in China in 1961. He is the sixth son in a family of seven boys. When he was very young, he lived in a poor farming village near Qingdao in northeast China. Then, one day, a visitor came to his school and chose Li Cunxin to join the Beijing Dance Academy. At the age of only 11, he left his home and went to live and study in Beijing, the capital city of China.

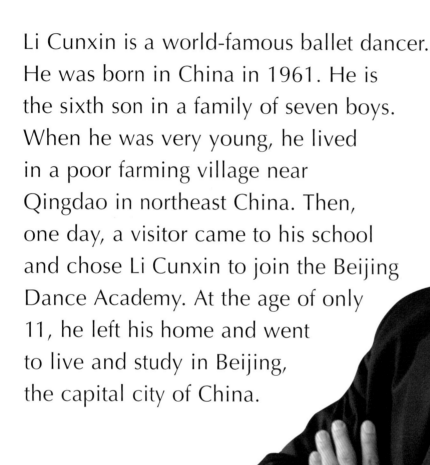

1961

Li Cunxin is born near Qingdao in northeast China.

1972

Li is chosen to attend ballet school at the Beijing Dance Academy.

July, 1979

Li is chosen to dance in the U.S.A. for six weeks with the Houston Ballet.

November, 1979

For the second time, the Chinese government gives Li permission to dance in the U.S.A.—this time for one year.

Setting the Scene

China in the 1960s and 1970s

Mao Zedong (right) was the leader
of the Communist Party in China.
China was under strict communist
rule in the 1960s and 1970s.
Communism is a way of organizing
a country where the houses,
businesses, land, and the food and
other products of the land belong
to the government or the community.

During this time, many people
in China were poor and starving,
especially those who lived
in the country.

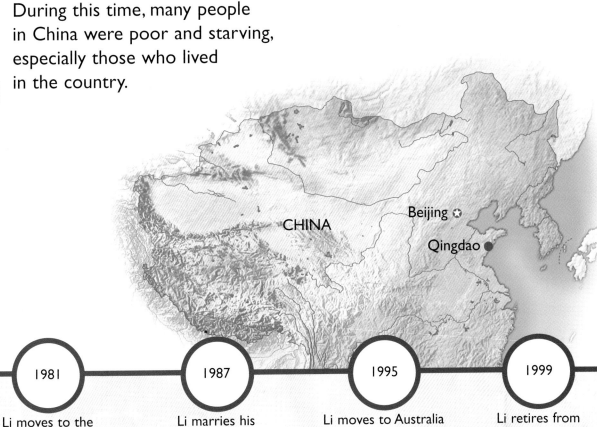

CHINA

Beijing ✪

Qingdao ●

1981
Li moves to the
U.S.A. By 1984,
he is a leading
dancer with the
Houston Ballet.

1987
Li marries his
Australian dance
partner, Mary
McKendry.

1995
Li moves to Australia
and becomes a lead
dancer with the
Australian Ballet.

1999
Li retires from
dancing to begin a
career in business.

5

Village Life

Li lived with his six brothers and his extended family. His father worked six days a week, and his mother cared for the family and worked in the fields. There was never enough food to go around, and Li was often hungry. At mealtimes, he wanted to grab the food and eat quickly, but he always waited for his parents and the other adults in his family to eat first.

extended family a family living together that can include grandparents, aunts, uncles, and cousins

The Chinese Communist Party came to power in 1949. In 1958, the Chairman of the Communist Party, Mao Zedong, began a plan called the Great Leap Forward. This plan was meant to improve life for the people of China and to provide for everyone equally. However, the plan didn't work. Instead, it caused food shortages everywhere, especially among those who lived in the country. Millions of people died from starvation.

The soil was poor quality in many parts of China. Most families planted yams because they were the easiest food to grow.

A Good Family Name

Although they were poor, Li and his brothers were taught family pride from a young age. Li learned an important lesson one day when he took his friend's new toy car. He told his niang (mother) he had found it on the street, but she knew he wasn't telling the truth. She was so ashamed. She marched Li back to his friend's house to return the car and to apologize.

apologize to say you are sorry

> *"Despite our poverty, our parents always taught us to have... honesty and pride."*
> **—Li Cunxin**

Traditionally, family life has always been very important to Chinese people. Children have great respect for their parents. As Li was growing up, he knew that his *niang* and *dia* (father) went without many things so they could provide for their seven sons.

Li is second from the left in the above photograph. He is pictured with his mother and six brothers.

respect placing a high value on
someone or something

Escaping the Well

*Li loved listening to stories. One day, his father
told him a Chinese tale. "A frog that lived in
a well tried hard to escape. He wanted to know
what was in the bigger world. Finally, he realized
that escaping from the well was impossible.
He was told to accept the fate into which
he was born."*

*Li sometimes felt like that frog. Life in his
village made him feel trapped. He dreamed
of a way out so that one day he could help
his family.*

Traditional Chinese tales have been told for many centuries in China. When writing developed, they were carved into bamboo. When the Chinese invented paper, the tales were written down. Many ancient tales and government records have been found.

The Chinese characters were cut into the bamboo and read from top to bottom.

ancient very old

What About That One?

One day, some officials were brought to Li's classroom. They were looking for children to join a ballet school. They walked up and down the rows of desks, watching the children as they sang. They chose one young girl.

The officials turned to leave the classroom. Suddenly, Li's teacher said, "What about that one?" That one was Li!

official a person who holds an important position
12   with an office, such as a government

In the late 1960s, it was compulsory for children to start school at the age of eight. However, when Li was eight, there was no room in the classroom for him. He had to wait until he was nine. When he finally started, he knew that his parents expected him to work hard and be a good student.

Above: Li's class photo, 1972. Li is seated in the front row, center. The scarves the boys are wearing show their support for Chairman Mao Zedong.

compulsory required by law

Months passed and nothing happened. Then, one day, a group of officials arrived at Li's home. Li had been chosen to join Madame Mao's Beijing Dance Academy. Li was very nervous. He had never heard of ballet. Besides that, he had never been away from his family and village. The people of his village provided a tractor for part of his journey to Beijing. Li's oldest brother took him to Qingdao, the first stop on the journey. They bounced all the way!

Chairman Mao's wife, Madame Mao, set up the Beijing Dance Academy to bring popular ballets, such as *Swan Lake*, to China. Ballets like this one had been banned for years in China, and many people had never had the chance to see them.

Li lived at the Beijing Dance Academy for seven years.

A Special Teacher

At first, Li was very lonely at the Beijing Dance Academy. He missed his family and his village. He was frightened of his teachers, and his dance classes were difficult and painful.

In his third year, Li developed a friendship with Teacher Xiao (sh OW). Teacher Xiao gave Li confidence and encouragement. Li worked hard and practiced hard. He wanted to please the teacher he loved.

confidence a strong belief in your own abilities

16

In 1975, Li's favorite teacher, Teacher Xiao, visited Li's home during the school vacation. Teacher Xiao was shocked at the living conditions in Li's village. Li agreed with him but said he didn't know how to help. Teacher Xiao told Li that he could help "by working hard and becoming the best dancer you can."

This photo of Li's village was taken in 2002. Li says that it has hardly changed since he lived there.

Giant Leaps

1977

Li couldn't take his eyes off the television screen. He was watching a video recording of the famous Russian ballet dancer Mikhail Baryshnikov. He couldn't believe how beautifully this man danced. He vowed to practice and practice until he, too, could leap and jump across the stage with such power and grace.

While he was at ballet school, Li was allowed to go home to visit his family only once a year. He loved seeing his beloved parents and brothers, but, in 1977, he decided to stay at school and practice his pirouettes. Li enjoyed his time alone, and he practiced all day. He set high goals for himself in the year ahead.

Li practiced alone and with his classmates. He worked hard to become the best ballet dancer he could.

pirouette in ballet, a turn of the body on the point of the toe or the ball of the foot

Going to America

Li didn't know it, but a visit from an American ballet teacher was about to change his life forever. Ben Stevenson, from the Houston Ballet in Texas, chose Li as an exchange student. For the second time in his life, Li was to travel into the unknown. He was very excited.

In the 1970s, many Chinese people believed that the United States was their enemy. Li and his traveling companion, Zhang Weiqiang, were very nervous when they first arrived in America. They needn't have worried. They met many friendly people and very quickly adapted to a new way of life that they enjoyed. It was, however, very different from their life in China.

Li and Zhang Weiqiang went sightseeing in New York during their first trip to the U.S.A. in 1979.

adapt to grow comfortable with a new situation

Chosen by Chance

Li was chosen by chance from a large classroom of children to join the Beijing Dance Academy. From that moment, he worked hard at a career that would last more than twenty years. When he found something difficult, he practiced even harder. He became a principal dancer for the Houston Ballet and then the Australian Ballet. He proved that hard work can lead to great success.

In 1999, Li traded his ballet shoes for a briefcase and retired from dancing. He now works in the business world in Melbourne, Australia.

principal one of the most important, or main, dancers in a dance company

More Famous Ballet Dancers

Mikhail Baryshnikov (1948–) was one of Russia's and the world's leading ballet dancers. He danced in many principal roles and then formed his own company.

Dame Margot Fonteyn (1919–1991) was known as the greatest British ballet dancer ever. In 1962, she formed a partnership with Rudolf Nureyev, a famous Russian ballet dancer.

Anna Pavlova (1881–1931) was a small, gentle, Russian dancer known as the "Dying Swan," after a dance she performed all over the world.

Anna Pavlova

What If?

Li Cunxin's teacher pointed him out to Beijing ballet officials as they were leaving his class one day. What if Li hadn't been chosen to join Madame Mao's Beijing Dance Academy? Do you think he would have spent his life in the village like his brothers? Or do you think he would have found another way to "escape the well"?

How did Li show determination as he learned to dance?

Index

determination a drive to succeed